Journey to Freedom®

W. E. B. DU BOIS

BY DON TROY

"THERE IS IN THIS WORLD NO
SUCH FORCE AS THE FORCE OF
A MAN DETERMINED TO RISE.
THE HUMAN SOUL CANNOT BE
PERMANENTLY CHAINED."

~ W. E. B. DU BOIS ~

Cover and page 4 caption:
W. E. B. Du Bois pictured
around 1918

Content Consultant:
Dr. Robert W. Williams,
Political Science,
Bennett College

Published in the United States of America by The Child's World®
1980 Lookout Drive, Mankato, MN 56003-1705
800-599-READ • www.childsworld.com

ACKNOWLEDGEMENTS

The Child's World®: Mary Berendes, Publishing Director
The Design Lab: Kathleen Petelinsek, Design; Gregory Lindholm, Page Production
Red Line Editorial: Amy Van Zee, Editorial Direction

PHOTOS

Cover and page 4: C. M. Battey/Stringer/Getty Images

Interior: Courtesy of the Special Collections Department, W.E.B. Du Bois Library, University of
Massachusetts Amherst, 5, 7, 9, 10, 11, 12, 15, 16, 20, 21, 26, 27; North Wind Picture Archives,
6; Library of Congress, 8, 13; Bettmann/Corbis, 17, 18, 23, 25; Underwood & Underwood/
Corbis, 19; Jean-Jacques Levy/AP Images, 22

LIBRARY OF CONGRESS CATALOGING-IN-PUBLICATION DATA

Troy, Don.
  W.E.B. Du Bois / by Don Troy.
    p. cm. — (Journey to freedom)
  Includes bibliographical references and index.
  ISBN 978-1-60253-140-6 (library bound : alk. paper)
  1. Du Bois, W. E. B. (William Edward Burghardt), 1868–1963—Juvenile literature. 2. African
Americans—Biography—Juvenile literature. 3. African American intellectuals—Biography—
Juvenile literature. 4. African American civil rights workers—Biography—Juvenile literature. I.
Title. II. Series.
  E185.97.D73T78 200–
  303.48'4092—dc22
  [B]

                        2009003654

CONTENTS

William and his mother,
Mary Sylvina, shortly
after his birth

Chapter One

BORN IN THE NORTH

 illiam Edward Burghardt Du Bois
was born in Great Barrington,
Massachusetts, on February 23, 1868.
It was an important time in U.S.
history. The U.S. Civil War had ended only three
years earlier. The entire country was going through
tremendous changes.

The Civil War had been a long, bitter fight
between the nation's Southern and Northern states.
It began when seven Southern states chose to
secede, or withdraw, from the United States. They
wanted to form their own country. One reason
these states left the **Union** was because Northern
leaders wanted to outlaw **slavery**.

Since the 1600s, many southerners had enslaved Africans to work their fields, care for their homes, and do other jobs asked of them—all without pay. Slaves were considered possessions. White southerners bought and sold slaves like cattle. Some northerners possessed slaves, but there were fewer slave owners in the North than in the South. In 1865, the North won the Civil War. Slavery became illegal throughout the United States. But the end of slavery did not mean that blacks had equal rights.

When William was still a child, his father left. Although the Du Bois family was poor, William had a happy childhood. He lived with his mother and was

Southern General Robert E. Lee signs papers of surrender at the Appomattox Court House in 1865.

close to his aunts. He was smart, fast, and athletic, and was a leader among the boys in his small town. When he was old enough, William had part-time jobs to earn money for his family. Although the North was relatively **integrated** compared to the South, William knew he did not always have the same opportunities as his white friends.

W. E. B. Du Bois in 1872

William was an excellent student. He graduated from high school in 1884 with top grades. He had always dreamed of attending Harvard University. But his family could not afford it. A friend who was a minister arranged for William to attend Fisk University instead.

Fisk University was a school for blacks located in the southern state of Tennessee. William's family worried about sending him to the South. The South had strict **segregation** laws. Blacks and whites were kept apart and treated differently. Nevertheless, William decided to take advantage of the opportunity to attend college. He packed his belongings and traveled to the South.

Students gather in the library at Fisk University.

While he attended Fisk University, William wrote for the school magazine, the Fisk Herald. *He was also the magazine's editor.*

William studied hard at Fisk. He also devoted some of his free time to teaching black children at nearby country schools. The people he met in these small southern communities were different from the families of Great Barrington, Massachusetts.

William was saddened by the poverty that was so common among blacks in the South. The segregation laws meant blacks could not attend the better-funded white schools. Blacks were kept from the best jobs, and many couldn't find work. Black men had been granted the right to vote in 1870, but whites often threatened them if they attempted to vote. Blacks couldn't eat in the same restaurants or use the same restrooms as whites.

More disturbing were the stories of blacks who were violently mistreated. Sometimes whites burned down the homes of black families. Other times, whites beat or even murdered blacks. At the time, **lynching** was a common practice in the South. When blacks were murdered, no one was arrested or punished. Slavery was illegal, but blacks still did not have basic **civil rights**.

William excelled in his college courses, but he learned more lessons than just those taught in the classroom. The more he discovered about the injustices blacks suffered, the prouder he became of his heritage. William believed that if blacks could remain strong under the most terrible conditions, they might achieve equality. He encouraged his classmates and others in the community to unite against **prejudice**. The rest of William's life would be dedicated to this cause.

Fisk University students and staff in 1887

Chapter Two

TO ACHIEVE EQUALITY

 n 1888, Du Bois graduated from
Fisk with honors. Harvard University
offered him a **scholarship**. In 1890,
he graduated from Harvard with
honors and a second college degree. Du Bois was
encouraged to learn more about the history of
slavery and of his people, so he decided to stay and
continue studying at Harvard.

During his years at Harvard, Du Bois
developed his theory that **racism** was caused by
ignorance. Du Bois decided to educate white
Americans about blacks. He intended to prove
that blacks were not **inferior**, as many whites
believed. Du Bois was convinced that if the United
States offered all its people equal rights and a good
education, the entire nation would be successful.

W. E. B. Du Bois, his wife Nina, and their son

In 1895, Du Bois completed his studies, which included time as a student in Germany. He was the first black student to receive a PhD from Harvard. Du Bois was one of the most highly educated Americans of his day, but no white university would hire him as a teacher. Du Bois finally found a job teaching Latin and Greek at Wilberforce University, a small school for blacks in Ohio. At Wilberforce, Du Bois met and married his first wife, a student named Nina Gomer.

Du Bois took the job at Wilberforce because he had to earn a living. But he did not plan to spend his life teaching. He wanted to do many other things with his education. He wanted to dedicate himself to achieving a better life for blacks.

After Wilberforce, Du Bois took a position at the University of Pennsylvania. There, he studied the black community in the city of Philadelphia. Du Bois

Du Bois married Nina Gomer in 1896. They remained married until she died in 1950.

returned to the South in 1897 with Nina to teach history at Georgia's Atlanta University. The university asked him to conduct research about blacks. Du Bois believed this was the chance to prove through scientific research that blacks were not inferior. Du Bois wrote many research papers about his findings.

His studies showed that like people everywhere, blacks were shaped by their history, their living conditions, and their education. Given equal opportunities, black people learned just as quickly and could achieve just as much as any other human.

Not everyone accepted Du Bois's findings, however. Some people did not want to believe that blacks were equal to whites. But other people welcomed and

W. E. B. Du Bois at Atlanta University

accepted his findings. Du Bois gave speeches and wrote articles that presented blacks and whites as equal human beings. But segregation and racism did not go away. His books were on the shelves of public libraries, but southern libraries wouldn't let him inside the door because he was black. Du Bois was invited to speak before members of Congress, but he couldn't ride the whites-only train to get there.

In 1903, Du Bois wrote a book of essays called *The Souls of Black Folk.* It said that the most serious problem in twentieth-century America was the separation of whites and blacks. Du Bois became the voice of protest against segregation and racism in the United States.

Booker T. Washington around 1903

One of the essays in Du Bois's book criticized Booker T. Washington, a black leader who was respected by both blacks and whites. Washington felt it was important that blacks have food, shelter, and good jobs. Washington thought these things were more important than equality or integration. He believed equality would come naturally if blacks simply proved themselves to be intelligent and hardworking.

Booker T. Washington was born into slavery in 1856. He founded the Tuskegee Institute that trained blacks to help them find jobs. Students learned skills such as cooking and blacksmithing, but they did not have an opportunity to study history, languages, or science.

In a famous 1895 speech in Atlanta, Washington encouraged blacks to accept segregation—for the time being—in exchange for education and jobs. He was convinced that over time, blacks would earn respect. Washington believed that blacks first needed basic necessities in order to live. Some people later called the speech the Atlanta Compromise.

Du Bois thought black students deserved more. "We want our children trained as intelligent human beings should be," he said, "and we will fight for all time against any proposal to educate black boys and girls simply as servants and underlings, or simply for the use of other peoples. They have a right to know, to think, to aspire."

As time went on, Washington continued to teach that people should not become discouraged about racial inequality. Du Bois was convinced that a new approach was necessary. He felt that Washington's acceptance of segregation was no longer the right approach. Du Bois believed that blacks must demand equal treatment. He encouraged people to protest and to take action.

In 1905, Du Bois organized the Niagara Movement. This was a meeting of black businesspeople, teachers, and ministers. It was held in Niagara Falls, Canada. The organization primarily dedicated itself to attacking Washington's ideas of accepting segregation.

The founders of the
Niagara Movement pose
in a photographer's studio
in front of a backdrop of
Niagara Falls in 1905.

Chapter Three

A NATIONAL ASSOCIATION

he battle between Washington and Du Bois continued. Du Bois also began to have trouble at Atlanta University. He knew that his beliefs were unpopular there. Du Bois began to believe that the university would receive more money from donors if he left. In 1910, Du Bois left his position at the school.

The members of the Niagara Movement united once again. They joined with other groups, including white organizations, and formed the National Association for the Advancement of Colored People (NAACP) in 1909. This new organization would play a powerful role in the battle for black civil rights throughout the twentieth century.

Du Bois became the NAACP's director of publications and research. He moved to Harlem, New York. For almost 25 years he edited the NAACP magazine the *Crisis*.

The *Crisis* was dedicated to the fight against segregation and racism. The *Crisis* staff investigated the ongoing mistreatment of blacks. Du Bois learned that black soldiers were being mistreated on French battlefields during World War I. When the war ended, Du Bois went to Europe to investigate and was shocked by what he learned.

He discovered a French government document titled "Secret Information Concerning Black American Troops." Du Bois published it in the *Crisis*. The document told French officers how to treat black U.S. soldiers:

> *"The black man is regarded by the white American as an inferior being. . . . We must prevent the rise of any pronounced degree of intimacy between French officers and black officers. . . . We must not commend too highly the black American troops, particularly in the presence of (white) Americans."*

When the NAACP first formed, it focused on creating laws that would make lynching and other violent acts against blacks illegal. The group also wanted to create laws that would eliminate **discrimination** *against blacks who wanted jobs.*

The cover of the first issue of the *Crisis*, published in 1910

W. E. B. Du Bois
in 1915

The *Crisis* sold 125,000 copies of the issue before the government directed the United States Post Office to stop delivering it. Government officials were deciding whether to **suppress** it. Government agents visited the NAACP offices looking for those who published the magazine. When the agents asked Du Bois what his organization was fighting for, Du Bois answered that they wanted the U.S. Constitution to be carried out. The *Crisis* had become one of the most important black magazines in the country.

Black artists drew the covers for the *Crisis*, and black authors wrote its poems, stories, and news articles. Du Bois wrote the "Men of the Month" section that featured prominent blacks. Du Bois saw the magazine as a place to discuss the NAACP and to tell the country what the group was trying to achieve.

During his years at the NAACP, Du Bois also began to openly promote **Pan-Africanism**. Pan-Africanism is the belief that all people of African descent have a common background and should cooperate with one another. Du Bois encouraged blacks in Africa, the United States, and other nations to consider themselves as one people. He thought they should strive to achieve equality and justice wherever they lived.

Over time, Du Bois began to have difficulties with other leaders at the NAACP. He wanted complete control of the content of the *Crisis,* but others at the

NAACP would not give up their power. Then, during the 1930s, millions of Americans found themselves unemployed during the **Great Depression**. In Harlem, where Du Bois lived, many people lost their homes and went hungry.

Du Bois felt that if blacks were to survive, they needed a new plan. He proposed they band together and form **cooperatives** in which blacks would start their own factories, farms, and businesses—separate from white communities. Blacks would do the work, and blacks would share the profits.

Du Bois published this idea in the *Crisis*. Other NAACP leaders disagreed with him, however. The NAACP promoted integration, but Du Bois's idea of black cooperatives was another form of segregation instead. Du Bois resigned from the NAACP in 1934.

Between 1919 and 1927, with the NAACP's support, Du Bois helped organize four Pan-African conferences with attendees from around the world.

W. E. B. Du Bois (back, right) at the *Crisis* office

Chapter Four

A DECADE OF WRITING

u Bois was 66 years old when he left the NAACP. He was at an age when many people retire. He chose instead to return to Atlanta University. During the ten years that followed, he wrote a number of his most important works.

In 1935, Du Bois wrote *Black **Reconstruction***. This book exposed some false information that had been published about blacks by white writers and historians. Many white historians had claimed that freed slaves were ignorant and dishonest. The writers argued that freedom was dangerous for such "inferior beings." They claimed "lazy" freed slaves who refused to work and caused trouble for white people made Reconstruction difficult.

Such views, written by respected white southern scholars, were used to enforce segregation laws.

Du Bois exposed these untruths in his book. He described the vital contributions of blacks during the South's recovery after the U.S. Civil War. He explained that within five years of the war's end, the cotton crop was fully restored. Within ten years, crops were stronger than ever. Du Bois argued that the South's economy recovered quickly—even without the free labor the slaves had provided.

In 1940, Du Bois started *Phylon*, a magazine dedicated to black race and culture issues. In the same year, he also published *Dusk of Dawn,* an autobiography.

In 1944, Du Bois faced more trouble at Atlanta University. Some other members of the University staff did not like all of his ideas. NAACP leaders heard what happened and invited Du Bois to return to the organization as the director of research. They encouraged him to devote his time and efforts to race issues in foreign lands.

After leaving Atlanta University, Du Bois published two books about the African continent, *Color and **Democracy*** and *The World and Africa.* For most of his career, Du Bois had protested against the existence of

W. E. B. Du Bois at Spelman College, an Atlanta college for black women, in 1938

Du Bois was dedicated to helping children overcome stereotypes. There was even an annual "children's issue" of the Crisis. *These issues introduced children to black heroes and encouraged children to act with honor and integrity.*

Three Africans who attended the Pan-African Congress later became the first prime ministers of Ghana, Kenya, and Nigeria. Those nations won independence in the following decades.

European colonies in Africa. Across the continent, European nations had used military power to take over huge expanses of land. Much of northern Africa, for example, was part of the French West Africa colony. England also colonized much of eastern Africa.

In 1945, Du Bois was involved in a new Pan-African Congress in England. The meeting was a success, and important black leaders from nations around the world attended.

W. E. B. Du Bois (left) and artist Pablo Picasso attend a peace conference in Paris in 1949.

W. E. B. Du Bois with his second wife, Shirley Graham, in 1951

Chapter Five

AN AFRICAN ENDING

n 1950, Du Bois's wife Nina died. In 1951, he married Shirley Graham. Graham was a writer and a political activist. The two shared many beliefs.

In the following years, Du Bois thought about the six decades he had spent fighting racism. He saw little progress. The United States was a democracy and should, therefore, offer all of its citizens equal rights. Black Americans, however, continued to be discriminated against nearly 200 years after the U.S. Constitution was written.

For many years, Du Bois had been studying the ideals of **communism**. Communism is a form of government that attempts to make all people equal. Ideally, no one in a communist society is richer than anyone else, and no one is judged by skin color. Communist leaders seriously discourage the practice of religion as well. They believe that religion causes disagreements between people with differing views.

In the 1950s, the United States was in the middle of the cold war with communist nations. Communism challenged the ideals on which the U.S. Constitution was based. Anticommunist feelings were strong.

Du Bois began to speak publicly in favor of communism. In 1951, shortly before he turned 83, he was arrested and charged with being a communist spy. There was no evidence to support the charges, so he was found not guilty. But his reputation was badly damaged. Publishers would not accept what Du Bois wrote, and no one invited him to speak. Some people still look down on his ideas because of his communist connections.

Although the United States tried to forget Du Bois, a few newly independent African nations did not. African leaders called him for advice. The president of Ghana, Kwame Nkrumah (**kwah**-mee en-**kroo**-muh), invited Du Bois to his country. Nkrumah called him a "friend and father," and asked him to work on the *Encyclopedia Africana.* Du Bois, who was 93 years old, accepted the invitation.

In 1963, Du Bois proudly became a citizen of Ghana. He said, "My great grandfather was carried away in chains from the Gulf of Guinea. I have returned that my dust shall mingle with the dust of my forefathers."

> *The cold war started after World War II. It was a time of tension between communist and non-communist nations. The two main countries involved in the cold war were the United States and the Soviet Union.*

Kwame Nkrumah, the first president of Ghana

On August 27, 1963, W. E. B. Du Bois died in Ghana. He was 95 years old. An honor guard carried his flag-draped coffin to the shore where he would be buried. It was a place close to an old slave-shipping port, where many Africans had been shipped to North America and forced into slavery. Du Bois died a citizen of a young African nation, a nation that could thank him for his commitment to freedom and equality for blacks around the world.

Du Bois's vision for an African encyclopedia inspired two projects. Africana: The Encyclopedia of the African and African American Experience *was published in 1999. A group in Ghana has started a set of 20 volumes named* Encyclopaedia Africana: Dictionary of African Biography.

W. E. B. Du Bois (center), Shirley Graham (right), and Kwame Nkrumah (left) in 1960

The civil rights movement occurred during the 1950s and 1960s. It was a time when many in the United States were rallying for equal rights for black people.

In the United States, one day after Du Bois's death, a civil rights march was held in Washington DC. One speaker at the event was a young black leader, Dr. Martin Luther King Jr. He was 60 years younger than Du Bois. Dr. King told how Du Bois rallied against the idea that black Americans were inferior to whites. Dr. King's words honored Du Bois as a fighter of injustice.

Dr. King respected the works of W. E. B. Du Bois and recognized his contributions to the civil rights cause. Without the lifelong efforts of Du Bois, the civil rights movement—and all the steps taken toward true equality for blacks—might never have occurred.

W. E. B. Du Bois was a champion for the rights of black people around the world.

TIME LINE

1860   1880   1890   1900

1865
The U.S. Civil War ends.

1868
William Edward Burghardt Du Bois is born on February 23 in Great Barrington, Massachusetts.

1888
Du Bois graduates with honors from Fisk University.

1890
Du Bois graduates from Harvard University with honors and a second university degree.

1895
Du Bois is the first black student to earn a PhD from Harvard University. He accepts a teaching position at Wilberforce University in Ohio.

1903
Du Bois's book *The Souls of Black Folk* is published.

1905
The Niagara Movement meets to organize and to protest the segregation of blacks and whites.

1909
The NAACP is formed. Du Bois is the editor of the organization's magazine, the *Crisis*.

1919–1927
Du Bois helps organize Pan-African congresses, encouraging people of African descent to unite.

1934
Du Bois resigns from the NAACP and his position at the *Crisis*. He returns to Atlanta University to write and teach.

1935
Du Bois writes *Black Reconstruction*.

1944
Du Bois returns to the NAACP as its director of research.

1945
Du Bois is involved in a new Pan-African Congress in England.

1951
Du Bois is arrested under suspicion of being a communist spy. He is found not guilty.

1961
Du Bois accepts Kwame Nkrumah's invitation to come to Ghana.

1963
Du Bois becomes a citizen of Ghana. He dies on August 27 in his new country.

Glossary

amendment
(uh-**mend**-munt)
An amendment is a change that is made to a law or legal document. The Thirteenth Amendment made slavery illegal.

civil rights
(**siv**-il **rites**)
Civil rights are personal freedoms that belong to all U.S. citizens. Du Bois was an important person in the fight for civil rights.

communism
(**kom**-yuh-niz-uhm)
Communism is a form of government that allows for all land, businesses, and profits to be shared by the government or community. Du Bois spoke positively about communism.

cooperatives
(koh-**op**-ur-uh-tivz)
Cooperatives are organizations that combine the efforts of many people united to work toward a common goal. Du Bois proposed that blacks form cooperatives in order to work together.

democracy
(di-**mok**-ruh-see)
A democracy is a type of government that allows the people to choose their leaders. Du Bois believed that in a democracy such as the United States, all citizens should have equal rights.

discrimination
(diss-krim-ih-**nay**-shun)
Discrimination is the unfair treatment of people based on differences of race, gender, religion, or culture. The NAACP wanted to lessen discrimination against black people.

Great Depression
(**grayt** dih-**presh**-un)
The Great Depression was a period of economic turmoil from 1929 through the early 1940s. During the Great Depression, many people did not have jobs.

inferior
(in-**feer**-ee-ur)
To be inferior is to be not as good. Du Bois wanted to prove that black people were not inferior to white people.

integrated
(**in**-tuh-gray-tuhd)
To be integrated is to have blacks and whites living together in the same community. Du Bois was born in the North, which was mostly integrated.

lynching
(**linch**-ing)
Lynching is putting a person to death by hanging without legal cause. Lynching was common in the South in the first half of the twentieth century.

Pan-Africanism
(pan **af**-ruh-kuhn-iz-um)
Pan-Africanism is a movement encouraging all people of African descent to cooperate with one another. Du Bois is referred to as the Father of Pan-Africanism.

prejudice
(**prej**-uh-diss)
A negative feeling or opinion about someone without just cause is prejudice. Throughout his life, Du Bois fought prejudice against blacks.

racism
(**ray**-sih-zum)
Racism is the belief that one race is superior to another. Du Bois identified racism in histories written by white authors.

Reconstruction
(ree-kuhn-**struhk**-shun)
Reconstruction was the period in the South after the U.S. Civil War in which the seceded states had to rebuild. Du Bois exposed false information about the role of blacks in the Reconstruction era.

scholarship
(**skahl**-ur-ship)
A scholarship is an award of money given to a successful student to be used toward his or her education. Du Bois was given a scholarship to attend Harvard.

secede
(sih-**seed**)
To secede is to formally withdraw from an organization, often to form another organization. The U.S. Civil War began when states chose to secede from the Union.

segregation
(seg-ruh-**gay**-shun)
Segregation is the act of keeping race, class, or ethnic groups apart. Du Bois disagreed with Booker T. Washington about segregation in the South.

slavery
(**slay**-vuh-ree)
Slavery is the practice of forcing a person or group of people to work without pay and treating them like property. Du Bois was born after slavery was made illegal in the United States.

suppress
(suh-**press**)
To suppress something is to stop it from happening. Government officials wanted to suppress the *Crisis*.

Union
(**yoon**-yuhn)
The Union is another name for the United States of America. The U.S. Civil War began when the Southern states separated themselves from the Union.

Further Information

Books

Bader, Bonnie. *Who Was Martin Luther King, Jr.?* New York: Grosset and Dunlap, 2007.

Blizin Gillis, Jennifer. *W. E. B. Du Bois.* Chicago: Heinemann, 2005.

Du Bois, W. E. B. *The Souls of Black Folk.* New York: Random House, 2005.

McWhorter, Diane. *A Dream of Freedom: The Civil Rights Movement from 1954 to 1968.* New York: Scholastic, 2004.

Swain, Gwenyth. *A Hunger For Learning: A Story About Booker T. Washington.* Minneapolis, MN: Lerner, 2005.

Videos

Against the Odds: The Artists of the Harlem Renaissance. PBS Home Video, 2006.

Black History: From Civil War Through Today. St. Clair Vision, 2008.

W. E. B. Du Bois: A Biography in Four Voices. California Newsreel, 1995.

Web Sites

Visit our Web page for links about W. E. B. Du Bois:

http://www.childsworld.com/links

NOTE TO PARENTS, TEACHERS, AND LIBRARIANS: We routinely verify our Web links to make sure they are safe, active sites—so encourage your readers to check them out!

Index